Contents

S0-AYA-036

Words in the glossary appear in **bold** type the first time they are used in the text.

The President of the United States

As our nation's leader, the president has a hard job. Although you know some things about the presidency, many facts may surprise you. Did you know the president throws the first pitch each baseball season? Keep reading to learn why and discover more unusual presidential facts!

William Howard Taft, the 27th president, started the practice of throwing the first pitch, and presidents have been doing it ever since.

Presidents and Their Terms of Office

name	dates in office	name	dates in office
1. George Washington	1789–1797	23. Benjamin Harrison	1889–1893
2. John Adams	1797–1801	24. Grover Cleveland	1893–1897
3. Thomas Jefferson	1801–1809	25. William McKinley	1897–1901
4. James Madison	1809–1817	26. Theodore Roosevelt	1901–1909
5. James Monroe	1817–1825	27. William Taft	1909–1913
6. John Quincy Adams	1825–1829	28. Woodrow Wilson	1913–1921
7. Andrew Jackson	1829–1837	29. Warren Harding	1921–1923
8. Martin Van Buren	1837–1841	30. Calvin Coolidge	1923–1929
9. William Henry Harrison	1841	31. Herbert Hoover	1929–1933
10. John Tyler	1841–1845	32. Franklin D. Roosevelt	1933–1945
11. James Polk	1845–1849	33. Harry Truman	1945–1953
12. Zachary Taylor	1849–1850	34. Dwight Eisenhower	1953–1961
13. Millard Fillmore	1850–1853	35. John F. Kennedy	1961–1963
14. Franklin Pierce	1853–1857	36. Lyndon Johnson	1963–1969
15. James Buchanan	1857–1861	37. Richard Nixon	1969–1974
16. Abraham Lincoln	1861–1865	38. Gerald Ford	1974–1977
17. Andrew Johnson	1865–1869	39. Jimmy Carter	1977–1981
18. Ulysses S. Grant	1869–1877	40. Ronald Reagan	1981–1989
19. Rutherford Hayes	1877–1881	41. George H. W. Bush	1989–1993
20. James Garfield	1881	42. Bill Clinton	1993–2001
21. Chester Arthur	1881–1885	43. George W. Bush	2001–2009
22. Grover Cleveland	1885–1889	44. Barack Obama	2009–present

Being President

FACT 1

Some presidents thought being president was a terrible job.

Have you ever wanted to be president? Before you decide, you might want to consider what some past presidents said about the job. George Washington said that becoming president made him feel like a prisoner going to his death! John Quincy Adams, the sixth president, said his years as president were the most miserable of his life. Martin Van Buren, the eighth president, said the happiest days of his life were the day he became president and the day he left office.

Washington made it clear that he would rather be at Mount Vernon, his farm in Virginia.

John Adams, the second president, found the job terrible. He said no one who had been president would congratulate a friend who became president.

7

FACT 2

There were eight presidents before George Washington.

George Washington was the first president elected after the states approved the **US Constitution**. But before the Constitution, the US government operated under the Articles of **Confederation**. Instead of a president like the one we have today, the Articles created the position "president of Congress."

The first person elected to the position of president of Congress was John Hanson. Some people say he should be considered our first president.

Presidents of Congress Under Articles of Confederation

name	term
John Hanson	1781–1782
Elias Boudinot	1782–1783
Thomas Mifflin	1783–1784
Richard Henry Lee	1784–1785
John Hancock	1785–1786
Nathaniel Gorham	1786–1787
Arthur St. Clair	1787–1788
Cyrus Griffin	1788–1789

FACT 3

If Alexander Hamilton had had his way, the president would serve for life.

Creating the presidency wasn't easy. The Constitution's writers argued about everything, including how long the president's term should be. They first agreed on a 7-year term. Then Alexander Hamilton suggested the president should serve for life. Finally, they approved the 4-year term we have today.

Alexander Hamilton was an important leader during the American Revolution and in the early years of the young United States. He served as the first secretary of the treasury under George Washington.

John Adams wanted people to address the president as "Your Highness."

Congress argued over the proper way to address the president. John Adams, Washington's vice president, suggested "Your Highness." But most members of Congress thought this sounded too much like a king. Today, the president is addressed as "Mr. President."

John Adams

11

FACT 5

Washington's salary was large enough to allow him to live like a king.

Congress thought the president should receive a large salary. Washington's salary was $25,000. That's about $1 million in today's money! And Washington liked the kind of expensive items a king would like.

Washington even bought leopard-skin robes for his horses!

Vice President
Joe Biden

Today, each candidate, or person running for president, chooses the person they want to be vice president.

President
Barack Obama

FACT 6

Washington didn't choose his vice president.

According to the system originally set up by the Constitution, the vice president was the person who received the second-most votes for president. It didn't matter whether the president and vice president got along or had the same ideas about government.

FACT 7

Eight of the first nine presidents were born in the British Empire, not the United States.

Of the first nine presidents, only Martin Van Buren was born after the **Declaration of Independence** was written. The United States didn't exist before this. The presidents born before the Declaration of Independence were born in British colonies and were British citizens.

George Washington, John Adams, Thomas Jefferson, James Madison, James Monroe, John Quincy Adams, Andrew Jackson, and William Henry Harrison were all born before 1776, when the Declaration of Independence was written.

Martin Van Buren

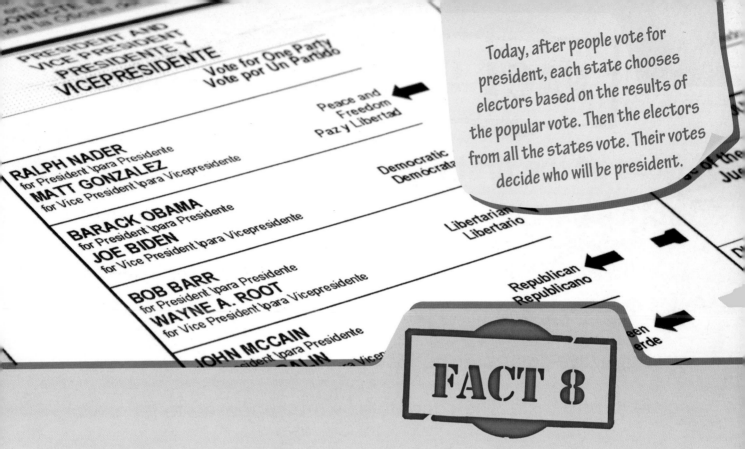

Today, after people vote for president, each state chooses electors based on the results of the popular vote. Then the electors from all the states vote. Their votes decide who will be president.

FACT 8

George Washington is the only president who was elected unanimously.

The Constitution calls for special **representatives** called electors to choose the president and vice president. Originally, each elector voted for two people. Washington was the only person to be elected **unanimously**. He received a vote from each of the 69 electors.

FACT 9

None of the first eight presidents took an active part in their campaign for president.

Today, presidential candidates travel around the country, give speeches, and meet people. But when our nation was young, active campaigning by the candidates was considered to be in bad taste. The candidates were supposed to let other people praise them and speak for them.

Prior to a presidential election, the candidates take part in debates. A debate shows Americans how candidates feel about important issues.

Thomas Jefferson

James Monroe

John Adams

Three early presidents died on July 4—the day we celebrate our nation's birthday.

Thomas Jefferson, James Monroe, and John Adams all died on July 4. Adams and Jefferson actually died on the same day—July 4, 1826. Monroe died 5 years later, in 1831. The 30th president, Calvin Coolidge, was born on July 4, 1872.

William Henry Harrison, the ninth president, was president for only 1 month.

As was usual, Harrison's **inauguration** on March 4, 1841, was held outside. Although it was very cold, he refused to wear a coat or gloves. He became ill the next day but soon recovered. He became sick again on March 27, 1841, and died on April 4, 1841. His presidency was the shortest ever.

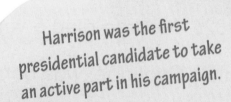

Harrison was the first presidential candidate to take an active part in his campaign.

Presidential Firsts

Abraham Lincoln was the first president to be photographed at his inauguration.

Photography was new in the 1800s. The earliest photograph was made in 1826. By the 1850s, everyone wanted their picture taken. Photographs of earlier presidents John Quincy Adams and William Henry Harrison survive, but they weren't taken at the presidents' inaugurations.

This photograph of Lincoln was taken on the day of his inauguration in 1861.

19

Victoria Woodhull was the first woman to run for president.

In 1870, Victoria Woodhull announced that she would run for president in the 1872 election. And women didn't even have the right to vote then! They wouldn't get the right to vote until 1920, when the Nineteenth **Amendment** was approved.

Woodhull ran for president under the Equal Rights Party, a party she had helped form.

Rutherford Hayes, the 19th president, had the first telephone put in the White House.

Hayes loved new **technology**, and he had a telephone put in the White House in 1879, just 3 years after its invention. He didn't get to use it often since there were so few telephones then. The White House phone number was 1.

Rutherford Hayes

Alexander Graham Bell

Hayes first used a telephone in 1877, when Alexander Graham Bell, the inventor of the telephone, showed it to him.

Warren Harding, the 29th president, was the first president to make a speech over the radio.

Although Harding died after only 2 years in office, he has several "firsts" to his credit. He was the first president to give a speech over the radio, the first to own a radio, and the first to ride to his inauguration in a car.

Harding was also the first president elected after women got the right to vote.

Today, any airplane the president rides in is called Air Force One.

FACT 16

Franklin Delano Roosevelt (FDR), the 32nd president, was the first to have his own airplane.

Theodore Roosevelt, the 26th president and a distant cousin of FDR, was the first president to fly in an airplane. But FDR was the first to have a special presidential airplane. It was called the Sacred Cow. FDR used it only once.

FACT 17

Nine presidents never attended college.

Today, we expect that the president has gone to college. But that wasn't always true. George Washington, Andrew Jackson, Martin Van Buren, Zachary Taylor, Millard Fillmore, Abraham Lincoln, Andrew Johnson, Grover Cleveland, and Harry Truman never went to college.

Before becoming president in 1945, Truman had been a farmer, soldier, salesman, judge, and senator.

Shown here, George W. Bush gives his second inaugural speech on January 20, 2005.

FACT 18

The longest inauguration speech ever given was more than 50 times as long as the shortest one.

George Washington gave the shortest inauguration speech. It lasted less than 2 minutes and had 133 words. William Henry Harrison, the ninth president, gave the longest. It lasted 1 hour and 45 minutes, and had 8,578 words!

FACT 19

Thomas Jefferson liked to greet ambassadors from other countries dressed in his pajamas.

Jefferson, the third president, thought Washington and John Adams had acted too much like kings. He believed there was no place in the new country for kings. To show he opposed kings and their fancy clothes, he met foreign **ambassadors** wearing his pajamas.

Andrew Merry, the British ambassador, was angry that he had dressed up in his fancy official clothes to meet Jefferson and Jefferson hadn't done the same.

The tallest president was a whole foot taller than the shortest president.

Abraham Lincoln was the tallest president at 6 feet, 4 inches (193 cm). James Madison was the shortest at 5 feet, 4 inches (162 cm). People of the time remarked on Madison's small size. It was especially noticeable since both Washington and Jefferson had been 6 feet, 2 inches (188 cm).

James Madison

27

Hail to the Chief

The president is one of the most powerful people in the world and has one of the hardest jobs. Some presidents have been true heroes. But whether they were heroes or not, all the presidents were human beings with flaws just like the rest of us. History is a lot more interesting when we learn fun and unusual facts. And we understand better, too.

Want to learn more fun facts about the presidents? Then check out the books and websites listed on page 31!

Barack Obama is the only US President from Hawaii.

Glossary

ambassador: someone sent by a group or country to speak for it in different places

amendment: a change made in the US Constitution

confederation: a league of people or states that support each other and act together

Declaration of Independence: the piece of writing in which the colonies said they were free from British rule

inauguration: a ceremony marking the start of someone's term in public office

representative: one who acts for a group of people

technology: the way people do something using tools and the tools that they use

unanimously: agreed on by everyone

US Constitution: the piece of writing that states the laws of the United States

For More Information

Books

Davis, Kenneth C. *Don't Know Much About the Presidents.* New York, NY: HarperCollins Publishers, 2009.

Katz, Susan. *The President's Stuck in the Bathtub: Poems About the Presidents.* New York, NY: Clarion Books, 2012.

Krull, Kathleen. *Lives of the Presidents: Fame, Shame (and What the Neighbors Thought).* Boston, MA: Harcourt Children's Books, 2011.

Websites

Fun Facts to Know About the White House Residents
www.scholastic.com/teachers/article/fun-facts-know-about-white-house-residents
Discover fun facts about all the presidents from Washington to George H. W. Bush.

Secrets About the Presidents
pbskids.org/wayback/prez/secrets/index.html
Find out surprising and unusual facts about presidents from Washington to Clinton.

U.S. Presidential Fun Facts
kids.nationalgeographic.com/kids/stories/peopleplaces/georgewashingtonicecream/
Did you know ice cream was one of George Washington's favorite foods? Learn more fun facts about presidents on this *National Geographic* website.

Index